50 SHADES OF BIPOLAR

50 SHADES OF BIPOLAR

Poems And Reflections
From A Twisted Mind

Stephen Bratakos

Library of Congress Control Number:		2014904156
ISBN:	Hardcover	978-1-4931-8096-7
	Softcover	978-1-4931-8097-4
	eBook	978-1-4931-8095-0

This book was printed in the United States of America.

Rev. date: 05/02/2014

To order additional copies of this book, contact:
Xlibris LLC
1-888-795-4274
www.Xlibris.com
Orders@Xlibris.com
541119

CONTENTS

CHAPTER 1

THE DISORDER

My name is Stephen Bratakos, I'm 29 years old, I'm a personal trainer and gym owner, and have lived in Southern California my whole life. This poem book is a reflection of my life while I was going through mania and depression. Yes, I am bi polar and was diagnosed at 28 years old. A little too late, but at least they caught it before I took my own life. My childhood was normal for a crazy kid :). My parents loved me and let me roam free, so in essence I grew up how I wanted inside a world with no structure. I was scared to death of my father, because we always fear the unknown; I had no idea what he was capable of. He is a great man and just did what he thought was right. My mother shielded me with unconditional love so I was too afraid to disappoint her. In other words I never got caught. Age 11 my parents divorced and I didn't see my mother for a few years after, there is more to that story then I can type. I only did bad things when I got what I thought was approval. My early 20's were interesting and full of stories and if I wanted I could write a whole novel on just that, but I'll keep it short and simple for this one. When I was finally diagnosed, the psychiatrist told me traumatic events in life can trigger the bi polar disorder rapidly. Bi polar disorder is mania and depression episodes that are uncontrollable; it's a mood disorder that's on its own clock. It's a disorder that leads usually to suicide or ruining your life with bad decisions although many of us are extremely successful with the uncalculated risks we dive into. From 23-26 years old I opened up 4 gyms, got married, had 2 beautiful boys, bought a house—tore it down, rebuilt it, lost it, bought 2 cars over 100k, lost both, lost two gyms, dropped out of college and was on my way to divorce and bankruptcy. My best friend lived with us in our new home and was imprisoned for an act which I can't discuss. This event was the straw that broke this camel's back. On top of it all I had to give away my dog which I never thought would hurt as much as it did, and to add insult to injury, I was addicted to xanax, muscle relaxers, paxil, and pain killers all at the same time. My daily Intake would be 2-3 of each with a glass of vodka. As a result, I developed gout, my kidneys were inflamed and I gained 48 lbs of fat. The doctors back then misdiagnosed me and I could have died. I walked into an empty house one day and told my wife, lets buy it, who cares if it's garbage, I can fix it myself, even though a contractor friend of ours told us, 100k to make it livable. Both bathrooms were sinking, no kitchen, the den was rotted, and no heat or air. The mania began from what I noticed at age 24 as I was going thru escrow. I used to tingle everyday with the worst anxiety I've ever had. I would tell people I feel like I need to jump out of my skin. I talked about suicide and murder like it was tea time with family. Finally escrow closed and I burst into the house that same hour with a sledge hammer and tore it down. I worked day and night putting my business last and the house first. I can only explain it as if I was possessed; not realizing mania can keep you thinking you're invincible. Mistakes are common but the big ones we pay for. I put 65k into the house in 4 months as the economy was crashing around us, I was 25 years old. I didn't see logic, just a chore. Lastly my dad was diagnosed with stage 3 colon cancer at the same time. So I believe those were enough reasons to get my disorder going. I'm probably missing things here and there but I've known people who break for much less. I went to India at the peak of my depression, after we lost the house and we just moved into an apartment. I left for almost 2 weeks and fate somehow kept Rachel away from coming on this trip. I went cold turkey and flushed all my pills while in India and that's when the mania hit me like a ton of bricks. I started lusting for another and another as I dropped 45 lbs in less than 6 weeks. I worked 7 days a week, balanced 2 kids and worked out 2-3 hours a day although I didn't even know my kids until Rachel discovered the disorder and I was medicated. It was as if a blindfold came off my face and I hadn't seen myself or my family in years. Sleep was forgotten, and my life spiraled out of control. I could convince myself of anything because under my clothes was a giant S and if I wanted to I could fly. I loved my wife for 11 years straight without a sign of doubt. The only thought running through my head at that time of disaster was I must keep her safe, who cares what happens to me. My feelings were mixed and I couldn't even speak of how I felt at the time, so I wrote it down. A five minute window of my higher brain talking as words flowed onto paper. Most of the time I wrote these poems or reflections while driving or *5am* in the morning or randomly waking out of sleep. After it all came out I was my crazy self again and writing was foreign. I passed every English class with a letter grade of C or D. I paid people to write my essays in college because I sounded like a 4th grader if I wrote them. Trust me I am no writer, the people who know me best can vouch for this. My brain would write about everything and nothing, whatever my mood was. Sometimes the poems were about friends, Rachel, me, people I barely met, girlfriends, girls I barely knew etc. On these next pages what you will find is bi polar me, forced to write from the depths of my soul, for I swear to you someone else is talking through me.

The Skinless Lion

I'm a lion without skin in a jungle with no king.
I eat from the finest trees and savor
the sweetest blood, for my enemies see no mane.
No one mammal can stop me in pursuit,
for death is always highest on the podium.

I've challenged myself into madness,
endured pain only a mother could share,
shown my teeth as the white has diminished
with death, but relapse is eminent.

I know no boundaries.
I create what I dream and destroy what I love.
I see the future for it is I that paints it.
Mindless are my thoughts and genius my language.
I crouch beside tall grass
preying on those that are filled with life.
Like a leach, I drink their spirit dry,
as the clouds moisten my tongue.

I cry when my eyes will no longer close
and smirk when my mind is silenced.
Hallucinations become supper on a plate too petite to hold.
My legacy will never decease for the insanity
surrounding it lingers on.

I roar when anger pricks me,
I run when the world is crushing me,
and attack my enemies when they think I'm dead,
for under my fur I hold scars of horror
no animal can swallow.

My jungle will burn at my hand
for the match I hold is the last in existence,
as I have burned each one the same.

I'm Only As Good As My Mood

Every second feels heavy.
With each tick of the clock
my life slowly unfolds before my
newborn eyes. Sprinting now walking,
I see in HD and my eyes have deceived me.

Once a lush forest filled with treasure and love,
now a desert filled with skulls and smoking ash,
never to be walked on again.

A magic trick with the utmost cruelty
while applauding as my heart breaks for the finale.
A blind man knows not what's ahead,
he's only as good as his guide
as for I am only as good as my mood.

For this sickness dwells deep in the mind
and offers visions one could only dream of,
for that inception was planted at birth
but would spawn into a rainbow of monsters.
A cure rest in the eye of the beholder,
a way out is not a bullet, but a friend.

A translucent idea that I chase
to the ends of the earth with no end in sight,
but in reality a dog chasing his tail
while punishment is extinct.

A relic I once held
has been dropped into the cracks of time,
keys I kept safe I have forfeited,
my life is gone while I hold a damp blindfold
watching my world die in the fire.
A friend will save you from harm,
a brother will risk his life for you,
but a soul mate will murder their happiness to save yours.

The Full MOOn

From a distance
a man saw his own reflection,
a nice tall slender figure.
He inches closer
and the image turns lopsided and fuzzy.
He winces and wipes his panicked eyes
and sees a monster.

Green eyes, clean shaved, and a beautiful smile.
This monster is a torturer of the mind,
leaving his victims desperate for love
and starved for his attention.
He knew what he was but never knew it,
for the mirror gave him unconditional depth.

The evils inside
were never meant to be unleashed.
Many moons it had been tamed
and his lifestyle hung in the norm.
One day it would breach the surface
as his hands grew claws
and face changed shape,
the full moon would become his enemy.

Nothing could slow him,
nothing could resist him,
he buried it deep, until he snapped!
He knew his name no longer,
his loved ones became prey
and the world he saw with hateful eyes
as he swore to devour its contents.

ManiA

Day one—it has a temper and attitude to build, buy and destroy.
It speeds up the hamster in my skull, and dopes me up with adrenaline.
Now I'm ready for any journey purchased from my imaginable fortune.

Day two—it has the consistency of web woven by the queen widow.
A web of lies, a web of deceit, a web that holds no boundaries
for it hangs in my subconscious.

Day three—bittersweet and rotten in the same recipe.
The ripest peach with the taste of sour milk.
We love like Gods but sin like soldiers.
We are trapped in a world of lust and greed.

Day four—the dragster now turns for the worst, depression.
With lack luster effects and a heart that weeps,
for we cannot see in this black cloud.
A mist, filled with remorse and pain,
it drapes on our heads like a soggy shirt,
sticking to one's body like honey.

Day five—*bed ridden, coma, exhausted from our worst enemy,
our mind. Fighting him like a bat straight out of hell.
We fight blind, swinging violently into the darkness.
We cannot win this battle but we can win the war
if we outsmart the conniving craftsman.
We need reinforcements, a silent horn blows
as we wait for our loved ones to complete the puzzle.
Hope rides the white horse, we wait, we fight, we tire,
we break, we stand again.*

Life's Cycle of Barbed Wire

We must ask ourselves, are we worth living. Taking space on this barren wasteland created by the unknown. Life's cycle can be treacherous, never knowing when deaths hand will greet us. Some prosper while others, who deserve too, fail.

Who decides prosperity, for is it not I. Obstacles with barbed edges seem impossible to walk thru, even more so with another on your shoulders. We end up wounding both, only meaning for one to take the fatal slice from Gods blade.

We seek purpose while others destroy and barricade our path. There are those in this sphere raging with gold and greatness but never sought out by the eyes of the creator. We are chosen from a sick tree that is wounded and dying as we humans keep on feeding it.

To fulfill ones destiny is to die at peace, to die alone is choice; to exit unwillingly is our creator at work cleaning up mistakes that were never in the master plans. We see death as sadness, when we can believe in an afterlife. We mourn when happiness is all they wished upon us.

Fate versus choice, sometimes one out-weighs the other when the end result was evil. For the righteous are always looked upon with fateful eyes while sin alone is blamed upon us. Maybe our path was set by fate for a dark purpose, so that the map of life can flow evenly. For one must believe in fate when something stolen from a locked safe is no longer theirs. At the same time one can only blame himself for the misery he has caused others while karma may set us free.

Love's Plane Ride

Please fasten your seat belts and prepare for takeoff.
Up ahead sunshine and clear skies, so grab your
gas masks and prepare for loves stench,
as it rots our insides with its twenty thousand foot drop.

Exits are located to your sides and to the front,
so brace yourself for the storm with no name.
For your raincoat cannot hold the acid
that drips from loves potion,
as holes burn into our fragile flesh.

Please return your seat to its upright position.
Once the turbulence has past, the future looks
promising as the plane lands smooth with no pilot,
for love's plane ride drifts alone with the cold wind.

Can we be happy without someone to indulge in
our nectar served first class. Can our demon thrive
without an angel to reprimand it. How can we crave love
when our plane has never reached that altitude.

Pleading in loves name as we spiral down towards the grey earth
as we wish it never to end. An invisible curse we will
never find, for we are the prey. A bitter sweet melody,
a fantastic joy ride with a cliff hanger ending.

Love's plane ride will take us to the unknown,
as we are blind when loves halo surrounds us.
When it lifts and sails away our eyes clear
and see where we really are.
Hell

Free World

Choice, we have it, we use it, and sometimes we cannot control it
for some elements are above it.
Choice is what separates us from the animals. It binds us to our
mistakes and accomplishments.
It gives us freedom
but can also enslave us into a glass box where escape becomes an
elusive dream.
Choice is the very thing we are born with but some may never
discover. We may live life without exercising this power to
choose.
Force will out rule choice, consequence will cease it, and love will
conquer it.
A decision to make, we can leave our shield up deflecting arrows
that are stained with loves spell, or we can leave our heart on our
sleeve exposing our weakness to the world.
Either way it will find you, like a disease that is airborne, you
won't know until it has filled your lungs and latched to your
heart.
It feeds off emotion, growing stronger each day, never letting us
recover.
Love is the one element that outweighs choice for it blinds us,
masking our inner demon so we can live in the moment.
Love is not choice, we do not decide who we love or when. If we
could choose love then world peace would be at our doorstep
and hell would be an illusion of the paranoid mind.
With choice we are all free, free in a world that chooses for us.

Wolves

The wolf, a hunter by nature. A majestic beast who scares with his teeth and hypnotizes with his moon shaped eyes. His gaze means death but has a calming presence amongst it.

He never shows fear even though his heart is racing. He slowly plans his next move while knowing the red lighting storm is up ahead. His language reads bodyguard as his mind whispers revenge, for those who wrong his blood line will be his next meal.

He takes care of many but cares only about one. His needs are first but always come last. Howling into the night, a call for lust while feeding his urge for retribution. He is untamed but at peace. He never strays from the pack for he is their fearless leader until another dethrones him.

Choice is not of the matter, for in his world there is none. He weeps at the thought of losing everything but has nothing to lose in essence. Everything can change in the blink of an eye, so for him he never blinks, at least for now.

The Impeccable Climb

A stranger to most, a friend to few, an enemy to no one except himself.
He climbs the endless mountain we humans call life. Many have
never stepped foot onto the sky scraper of rock and bones
and even fewer have ever made it to the invisible peak.

Once we engage we climb to reach the top never knowing
there isn't one. Close calls and death lurk behind us.
Freedom and motivation creeps slowly within us.

Happiness and peace always seems to be one step ahead,
always the better climber and never letting our hand grasp
with theirs. Our minds are one with the journey until
the clouds clear and we see where we really are,
an ant on the tallest ant hill, a dear in a field of wild lions,
a flower in a forest fire. Ready to meet our doom
before hope has ever crossed our brilliant mind.

Then a moment of silence we are able to see
the peak for a prompted second, Gorgeous.
We keep climbing with ferocity only to realize
we are similar to a hamster on a wheel,
running but never going forward.

We may accomplish turning water into gold,
creating life, building an empire,
but the endless fact remains, we are alone.
From start to finish our footsteps are many,
but will perish with silence for
life and death are lonely journeys.

Hanging from a harness that is
bounded to nothing but ourselves.
Truly the only way up is with
the sacrifice of another.

Superheroes

There are those who bleed through our windows to extinguish an accidental flame while their bodies deform with courage. Those who bite the bullet to keep our youth for theirs will perish.

Those who chase monsters that control fear in a world where peace has never existed. There are those who sacrifice themselves whole, for a religion that shows no truth.

Those who shed their skin so their seeds may walk proud on this earth. A mother will die slow so her son may live strong; a father will take a life, for vengeance is the badge he wears.

Heroes and villains are one in the same for its only unjust if your society believes it so.
Leave your mark and die in vain for one day we will call you a hero, the next someone else will take your crown of thorns for this gutless world we live in will always decide which team we play for.

I am neither, I am fair, I am true, I will do what I have too for I am my own society and within it, everyone's my enemy.

CHAPTER 2

LOVE????

My high school sweetheart, Rachel. We met in 10th grade and fell in love. I told her a couple months after dating that I would marry her. She was the only girl I'd ever been with and I was her first too. We grew up together, traveled the world, and shared laughs that will only die with us. She knows everything about me and she knows me better then I know myself. To have someone look you in the eye and tell you you're a stranger and a monster after 11 years is very confusing at a time when you're lost. We were the "American couple" and envy surrounded us everywhere we went. We had it all. Now, why would someone want to throw it away? I'm asking because I have no idea. My point is this disorder is stronger than anything I've felt before. The mania is so strong, that maybe a certain someone could carry a loaded gun on their lap for their daily commute and point it at anything and everything just because you're craving invincibility. Fear is a word that doesn't exist when you're manic, like my therapist said all I need is someone to provoke me when I'm high and off to prison. I saw Rachel as my enemy; I created a prison in my mind from which I was trying to escape. I would scream at her "I'm trapped, you trapped me!!!" She didn't understand and depression had taken over her body and mind. I wish she would have left me sooner because it's impossible to look at what I did to her. I will feel guilt the rest of my life even though it wasn't truly me, but the damage was done. I could watch her cry about us and feel nothing, I could see her in pain but I was blind, I was numb to everything and everyone. Therapy was interesting, as 3 different therapists told her let it go, it wasn't him doing it, he was sick, but it was me in the flesh hurting her but not me in spirit. I would never stoop that low by choice, and if u look at paper it reads—vanilla vanilla vanilla vanilla vanilla vanilla vanilla vanilla vanilla vanilla rockyroad Oreo blizzard. The graph doesn't lie. Second chances are not always given, and caution to those of you who may be at risk, don't wait until it's too late. After my heart finally broke and meds kicked in I began to feel and the words flowed and the sorrow and remorse was put into poems once again.

The Fog

I see you thru the fog, black dress—red lips; you taunt me with yo
and stab me with your walk. You have eyes for only me, but they nc
look my way. Passion fills this empty room as reality drifts. Your touc
 felt before, your body I've seen nude and your mouth I've sucked dr

Love we have no more, pain now feeds our lust, and regret fuels a broker
future. A feast I've had, and a feast I will now long for, as a wrath of grapes
 I have fed you, wine I have poured down your chin, and the finest cigars I
have breathed into your lungs. For romance was the cloud we walked and
passion the bridge we built.

The Fog, a fog that resides in my mind, for you're there but only in
memory. My deceitful eyes see your blurred figure but I no longer can
read you. My hands reach for your body but grasp your murky ghost.
Tears run down a wet cheek—I seek harder, I run faster, I scream your
name, but only echoes into the madness I dream with.
The fog has taken you from my soul for many moons ago they were
inseparable. My search continues until my mind wins and obliterates you
from it, leaving a cold empty frame that leans against my heart.

Perfect Stranger

Perfect stranger. You've known me for a lifetime but young and fragile we still are. You've known me in your day dreams, you've kept me safe when danger lurked from my tongue. You say the right things even if they're wrong.

You've kept me warm when I've never spoke the words cold. I glance at you once and you've seen me in another life, I glance twice and I'm stained with your beauty. You eat from my hand but I have nothing to give. You take nothing from me but everything.

You've watched me before from a distance, a distance not made of measurement but of time. You knew who I was before I knew myself; you saved your heart and readied it to break with mine.

Your skin though soft has become scarred with nightmares from a past, but will heal from a future you will create. You fight me with nothing but your mind, a battle not yet begun. You heal me with time for it is that very thing that has let me grow.

You've waited for something perfect but will settle for broken. You've known the future without knowing, and in it was I, your perfect stranger.

Wise With love

Your smile exudes the darkest empathy. Your hand heals while your tongue ages me. Your gaze, sharp, as if I were a rabbit, and you a hungry wolf. You carry the scent of flowers by day and by dawn your original scent blisters from your skin and sends me back to age seven.

Safe is a word I relate to you, comfort is the roof over your head and catering is what you bask me with. My mother has your drive; your mother has your good will. Together you are the women I wish to be held tight by, as my dying body embraces the last moments on this earth.

You've shown me how to read between the lines from a torn apart book and accept that life sometimes cannot give us what we ask of it. You substitute hate and death with love that showers me as I clean my body of your blood.

We grow together but you have been aged for centuries. The wisdom in your hands is greater than the knowledge in your mind. You seek me but I am broken, you fix me only to break again, and after I am in pieces you lift me with your loving grace knowing we both will fall.

I've loved your face since I've seen it glisten in the sun, I've loved your shattered insides since the first time my sweat was upon your lips as the moon beat down on my back.

You can never change me for the monster inside can only die by my hand. You can never lose me for I've already swallowed your heart whole. You can never fix me for I am not broken only scarred. Learn each other we will, give to one another we must, and die in loves name we shall.

For love is an elixir that carries the sweetest life and breaths the most painful death.

From Yesterday To Forever

From yesterday to forever . . .
Someone I've loved since I've kissed her in my dreams.
A dream that never ceased to exist until her lips grazed mine. A hand that held
mine in a time of uncertainty and confusion. A touch that calmed a raging storm.

How can one go on with life never knowing if loves arrow will ever pierce again?
Why waste such a good thing when it pampers us with pleasure and ahhhh.
Taking us to hidden places only few have ever been. Showing us hidden treasures
that many never knew existed.

A woman I've loved since the day her Carmel Candy Eyes were lit up by the sun
and stole my heart. She's a thief in the night taking from me a piece of my heart
with every cuddle, every kiss on the neck and every sigh of ecstasy released from her
soul. She has a swagger only few can match, a touch only one being can replicate,
and a kiss that none will ever suffice too.

A heart filled with bittersweet broken memories. A mind that thinks as one with
yours. Open arms that can accept you for whatever monster you are. She can
make time stop with her gaze, and time fly with her laugh. She's what every man
desires, she's what every man truly needs, and to have her is to be the luckiest man
in this loveless world.
To lose her, now that's something words can't describe.

The Auburn Candle

The pleasure is infinite as our eyes lock without a
key. Our lips touch as if we never met, kissing in a
soundless world as time lay dead in the closet.

> We hold one another tight as though fear
> were our blanket and panic our pillow. We
> rip apart sweaty clothes as though dollar
> bills stacked high in room built from our
> parents.

Lust builds as love shadows our touch; we seek sounds of
ecstasy as our ego builds itself higher.

> We are wild animals protecting a nest of secrets we both
> share. Heavy breath lies upon us, finger tips turn sharp as
> they pierce our dense skin.

Possessed with romance, as our eyes glow from an
auburn candle while passion drips onto each other's
chests.

> Side by side we reside heavy with awww, as we
> drift away in the night's mist.

The Puzzle Piece

Your hand will always fit in mine as if it were the missing puzzle piece in my life. Your lips will always remember mine as if they were a pair made to taste one another. Your skin will always fear a touch unknown and always crave a touch that has caressed it before.

Your eyes will always have a glimmer of hope, as eyes who've seen beyond them once before can speak love without saying a word. You've seen passion burn from my eyes as the cloud of lust became a storm, as we floated into the arms of the hurricane.

You will always crave a sensitive smirk over a cunning grin, for the little things in life reign over ignorance. You lay at peace but dream of war, for your past will never forgive you.

Comfort I give you, warmth I can provide you, and romance I dance around you as we fall over our heels in love. Alone in your bed, your eyes wide with confusion, for you yearn while my ghost bleeds your tears.

You'll always remember my laugh as it complimented yours and laugh you will, as yours will shadow another's. I only wish your heart to stay warm as it remembers my beat, for long ago we walked at peace in a rain that kept us warm as I held you tight whispering we can never die, for this is heaven.

sorRy foR beIng mE

Sorry for being me
as you lay there with white sheets that match your skin. The view is
foreign as street signs fill the void in the air. You cannot speak yet for
sorcery has cut your tongue. You dream for you have no choice, as your
delicate face is colored white and purple.

This chair is now my home as it engulfs my last memories. The reaper
stares from outside our frosted window tense with anticipation, as I build
a nest of saints around us for no army can shield his scythe. I now hold
you with grace for my hands carried the most vial anger.

You blur now and then for I cannot contain this guilt my chest holds with
a straw. Strange men in masks whisper to me but remain my enemies
until you breathe that sweet life we once savored. I've watched you as the
hair from your scalp has turned brittle, I have seen your ghost as I swore
revenge if it fled.

Hope was a word that kept me sane, for now my insanity will burn this
place and welcome us into the afterlife with your smile holding mine.
Nights become days and days become eternity as my thoughts are
constant in a mind that is broken. That night marked our homecoming
for love was our drug as our nostrils turned white with life.

The car I drove was never ready for the cliff that swallowed us. It should
be me that faces the reaper, it should be me that is dead to this holy
world which is bright with flames as for now I will walk away and burn
alive as my body melts into a puddle of your tears.

The Young Aged Couple

She breaks him without remorse, for she is taped together from a past that built her leaning empire. She tests his strengths for he is her superhero in a world without villains. She drowns him with slurs of aggression for he holds no truth in their kingdom forged from treachery.

She is the raging bull he once trapped with his red cape, he is her balance from their frictionless world, and in a heartbeat he'll rip out his soul to save hers. His speech is a map to nowhere but his intentions hold the key to happiness.

Break us once and forget the night, break us twice along with our hearts, break us thrice and we forget our names for she bears no witness to the madness that spews from their tongues as it latches like a disease that slows down a future that remains their past.

Their love burns eternal under the rain their storm creates. Young love will blossom into old friendship as they learn life's hardest lesson, one cannot make one happy until they have slit their throat of resentment spilling out the demons that wear their skin.

I Wish I Was You

Wish I was you.
Your sealed grace slows down time; your body moves
like a cold wind, your gaze can paralyze the walking.
Wish I was you.
You stare at death with happiness, you taste like candy
but you're sugarless, you glow in the darkest places.
Your voice is known to many but melts only one, you're
at the speed of light but you think in slow motion,
you're a clock without time written on its face.
Wish I was you.
You count the days backwards when you look forward,
you stop for no one but carry everyone, you mean
nothing to the world but you caress the gifts it's given
you. You're the dim flame that will never burn out,
you're the rain that comes when there's no drought,
you're a wolf in sheep's clothing but you never bite.
Wish I was you.
You sleep as if you never knew fear, you rise with a
bright glimmer in your eye, and you fall knowing you
will rise again. Death fears you, angel's envy you and
sin resides deep inside your faultless body. Before
it's gone you know what you have, letting go comes
with ease but it's never a first. You strive but you never
strain, you break only at your own hand, you love as if
the world was over, you think together but as one you
shall remain.
Wish I was you.

My Invisible Friend

*My invisible friend. There with me through the thick and thin though you
don't exist. Alone with me in my room when the tears became nothing
but a stain on a once loved cheek. There with me when the nights were
unbearable and death seemed the only known response for peace.
My friend whom I had not met but one day will have known my entire life.
There with me when the highs were a blissful glimpse into a reality not far
from fate and one lingering on a tainted thread that can only be cut with a
blade made of tears.
A future filled with happiness one can only dream about for you've seen
many of them. A happiness that does not come from within but from
laughter, adrenaline, highs and lows and the shear thought of being without
one another for we are bonded through fate.
My friend, my dear friend
where have you been hiding. In a place where man is forbidden to go, in a
place many seek their whole lives but never find. You've seen me grow but
have never fed me yet I've savored your spoon.
You've watched me love and break as your hand held mine while a pillow
was my comfort.
You are the air I breathe, you are the other half of me that has been lost for
centuries. You know me from within but a stranger from without, you share
with me your vision for I can taste you when my eyes close.
You've met my monsters and seen the dark side that I was born with yet you
show no fear, only acceptance. We fell from the same tree and blossomed
side by side with the universe as our fence.
For one day your face will greet mine, while I've waited to see your smile
and hear your voice as you have kept me safe my whole life. I've never been
alone for I have you.
My invisible friend*

CHAPTER 3

DEPRESSION IN THE DARK

Depression is a disease. It keeps us from being productive and twists our mind into doing unfulfilling work. It seems to run in our blood and keep coming back. I think pill treatments are only band aids. Many know depression but many cannot survive with it for too long. Bi polar depression comes in waves and mine usually lasted 1-3 weeks. 12 % body fat back to 18% and then back down again. That was my cycle. My depression wasn't as bad as the mania but while I was on that remedy of pills I would often black out at the gym while training or black out at home not remembering how I got there. Alcohol and pills are the worst thing for a bi polar, it's literally a recipe for death. I was lucky India happened, but at the same time I would lose my soul mate. Who knows why things happen the way they do. I used to believe in fate but now I believe in choice. We always blame something else then ourselves, it's easier this way. Mental disorders are a tough one, because no matter who we hurt, people want us to accept blame even though we're blind folded. I accept what I did and believe me all I want is to make it up. Most depression episodes would lead to heavy drinking or crying uncontrollably which is something I have never done! I can't remember crying since ninth grade when Rachel broke up with me for summer, and before that maybe when I was nine. I watched my childhood dog get put to sleep after our German Sheppard ripped her to shreds, never cried. Cancer, death, my wedding, my sons births with a crash cart c section, etc. never cried. It just wasn't in me, but when this damn disorder hit I would be crying while I was at the gym or driving or watching Friends, or hearing Celine Dion on the staticky radio. Now explain that if you don't know you're mentally unstable. The funny part is it's almost impossible to figure it out and my worst fear was going crazy. Emotions were as heavy as a semi and when they would hit I was laid out for weeks. And the sadness would build and there were no more tears to cry so my hand wrote it as the voices deep within came to life.

Misery in the Middle

My heart beats with yours yet intertwined with another's. My veins are stale and dry for you have cut me open with my own weapon. My tears have pooled and stained my clothes, as the tears she gently wipes away weep for your ghost.

> *My body tingles through the brass triangle as my mind fights a demon that wears your scent. I scream in terror as she whispers redemption while I dream of pain and beauty. Lost in love, found in friendship.*

Mixed with sugar and spice, for one cannot be whole while he carries an empty carcass in his suitcase. I loved her as deep as the rotting ocean could sink, I sang in my sleep for happiness was my hallucinogen.

> *Stories of a once romantic fairy tale, now shared in the trenches of broken dreams, for I speak of them with another as she writes her next chapter titled with another's name. I forgave myself as I punished everyone.*

I kiss her lips for I cannot remember your taste, my fingertips caress her spine as a daydream becomes a puzzle with your body trapped inside. With time I shall mend my ashes with glue from a past when purity haloed over our heads.

> *I will find peace from war and rebuild this home that does not exist. Visions mix with pleasure as your voice revisits, you speak to me void sound, but I can hear perfectly. "Let go." My grip is tight as I squeeze the breath from her body, while I forget your name and erase history from my burning eyes.*

What I Wouldn't Do

What I wouldn't do with a broken heart. I wouldn't set this house on fire for your deceit has painted it red with blood that drips off a metal blade.

I would never strangle you breathless for I love how you lie while your lips kiss mine with the uttermost passion.

I would never cut your eyes out for they have seen another's flesh while lust fueled a fire that will burn you into the afterlife.

I will never betray you with kindness for I have felt God's hand strike me down, as you will feel mine with no mercy.

I will never leave you behind for your ashes will hang from my neck as I weep tears of closure.

I will never let you free, for we have bonded our souls with chains and barbed wire that has no beginning or end, for I will make them suffer beyond this life.

I will never burn the flag of justice for no court can hold this raging beast as I spray yellow on a jury who befriended you.

I will never claim what is mine nor will I spit on your grave for you have haunted me into madness.

I will never let you down for I have swallowed your secrets whole as I will vomit them onto the world's network of filth.

I will never shadow you from above for you are my equal, as you speak tongues with a snake that has burrowed under this house and released its venom into our roots as we only grow sicker.

I will never live behind you, I will never lead another life, for I am your second and last in a world you created underneath me.

Priceless

Amazed, stunned and distraught at the same time. Her beauty is natural but of a different breed. Smart is what she appears, brilliant is the mask she wears and cunning is what she exudes.

Stubborn in her ways, an immovable brick when it comes to chance. She prepares for nothing, but is ready for everything this shallow world has. She's never convinced until her eyes gaze upon it and even then she's skeptical.

Being with her is bliss, living with her is stability, and having her as an equal is second to none. We strive for greatness, but leave behind something that's greater.

We will never know how much we care for something until it's gone. Once we destroy it, we try so hard to fix it but the directions are alienese.

It's a fact we must live with as the knife in our heart gently punctures every time we breathe. To win back something lost is to gain everything, to lose something priceless is to lose yourself.

Leap Then Run

1 . . . 2 . . . 3, leap.
A man in love but his path is clouded
with hazels and emeralds. Confused
and broken, he still pursues her.
Gorgeous and wounded, a deadly
combination for a woman who's being
hunted. He climbs the rooftops
shouting her name, but she responds
to no one. He traps her in a dream and
breaks through her wall of hurt. Trust
in another is something you cannot
find it has to be earned. They learn to
know each other from the inside, they
break one another, test each other's
anger. Always followed by the comfort
of touch and tears for two that are
broken can never fix one another.
The darkness grows, as my stomach
feels twisted. We sat on clouds in
the rain forest, and walked amongst
saints as one cannot see the devil
inside. My heart burns for yours, my
body the same, you warned me but my
eyes were too focused. Your blame,
your inner demon, they are no match
for my resilience. I will show you the
light, a way out of the cave and back
into the orange sun. Or may I leave
this forever and choose weakness for
I do not break, I am already in pieces.
I do not run for my legs are buried.
One question remains, is this real.
1 . . . 2 . . . 3, Run.

Guilt

Guilt, a bond that ties us to misery. Chaining us to sorrow and remorse. A lifetime of it can be the cruelest punishment bestowed on the living. There is no escape, only acceptance. Even then your world is engulfed with memories that whisper in your ear and dance before your eyes.

You can't run nor hide, only one way out you will find. No exit sign in the building, doors on fire and the windows barred.

Guilt, the very thing keeping man from chaos. It eats you from within and feasts on your tissuey brain.
You forgive yourself but find no sympathy, you seek it from another but their lips tell no truth.

You hear only words but feel nothing, you speak but say nothing. Locked in a dimension where time does not exist. Where you plead help, but none can.

A place you've set on fire but has never burned. Guilt, a reflection of one's self created by one's self to remember the monster they are for all eternity.

By a Thread

Hanging by a thread there was a man.
In one hand he holds a key, a key that can unlock
any door in life he wishes, but only alone may he enter.
In the other he holds a thread made of diamond, a thread which carries
children, a wife, and other living creatures. With this thread he may climb to
an impeccable summit, but only with the weight of the world residing on his
shoulders. For the thread will never break, but the man climbing
it may.
Hands will be callused so we may endure, broken but healed with time. His
hands have the power to take life as well as save it.
With each pull to the unfathomable peak
the man becomes stronger as he
weakens within.
Climbing the fortress may never have been a desire, but once we start the
journey turning back could be a fall from which our delicate minds
will never recover. Has any man breached the top
of what seems to be an endless journey.
Each thread we grasp
bears new life
but is every
journey
inevitably the same ending.
How does one know
which thread to hold onto when
so many dangle in front of him. Those who
choose never to grab hold will forfeit life's gifts.
Love, happiness, offspring, and a bond stronger than any mind
can explain in words. We only get one key and once we let go we fall
together.

Born Into 3

A girl born into 3 takes a lonely approach into the family that brought her into this world.

Her purpose, unknown.

She grows gracefully yet takes to a dark passenger that now consumes her. Fluid that poisons the brain while allowing her young demons to hold the wheel. Sorrow looms over her head as she enters adulthood.

Her purpose, unknown.

She runs with no end in sight, as the track behind her is caving in. She approaches insanities doorstep while keeping her smile intact. Her life now comes with a lock and key. A whirlwind of secrets and pain kept invisible,
as her laugh could melt a small room. She leaps for freedom as the bullet shows no scars. Darkness has turned to light and her path looks promising.

Her purpose, unknown.

Her journey slows to a halt as she is content with life's empty box. Blind with doubt and uncertainty, she lives as if fear was foreign. Void fills her soul, as deep fruitions of love are locked away in her heart with a key that vanishes as her acid devours it. She is now wiser and stronger in every aspect.

Her purpose, unknown.

One day a stranger finds her as they stare into a mirror that sees one. Vibrant and charismatic she is once again distracted from the void that has consumed her body and mind not knowing this person holds a key that she lost a long time ago. Neither knows what the other holds but in a split second they are connected by the heavy hands of fate.

Day by day she grows more intrigued. Pandora's Box which had been filled with memories and life has now been opened and pours into the other. The stranger shows her the world through his wide eyes as she straps on her parachute. Who knew that the same world we share looks unknown through the eyes of another. She bonds with him sharing her darkest secrets as if they were still alive. The stranger balances her for the beam is heavy on one side. She teaches him, shows him a calmer side of life, slows the storm that rages deep inside him.

Her purpose is now known, a free spirit that can spare her soul to save another's.

My Leaking Heart

A broken heart, otherwise known as the hand of god ripping your
intestines out as the vultures creep in. A dull rusted knife stabbing
your aortic valve until blood fills your stomach.
Tears that never stop falling until your skin is raw.
A heart beat that is dull but heavy. Heavy enough to weigh us down
and hang our heads. Is one able to recover from such pain, only time
will deliver that note.
Ache that fills the body with poison, a poison that soaks in muscles
and restricts our veins. Time will heal all, but time is also death, can
they be the same?
Can time mend but also destroy. We find ways to heal with friends,
leisure and material, but it's only band aides that cover a gash that
leaks eternally.
A broken heart, human's deepest pain.
A path to the dark side, a path to revenge, a path to the other side of
this two faced world, for many of us never recover to normalcy again.

Rich

We dream in diamonds and gold. We see with greedy eyes and point with a
jaded tip for life's remnants will not suffice.
We speak in French when our taste buds have
only sampled home cooked. We lie
to our neighbor with rims
and castles
much
loftier then
societies allowance
while our conscious hides
the truth. We play all in, even though
the chips read low. Mistakes are in the bank
and the future is in the hand of a bookie. Our family
grows wide as we feed them with foreign cuisine. Hunger pains welcome us
as an everyday occurrence as morality
strikes out. Pretend we must, survive we shall.
In the end we take everything only our
minds can remember.
Our treasures rot,
our silver becomes rusted.
For in this lifetime our worth is not
defined from size or caliber, but from the people
you sacrifice for it,
for they are the
true riches.

Lost

My heart is lost with you. Only the shadows of the underworld can hear its faint beat. Timeless my life has become, effortless are my cries for help. You have shown me a new path with force and given me a different perspective for my old one was of death and sadness.

You're bonded to me forever but I've lost you in this lifetime as our hands no longer feel one another's grace. A wondering soul in loves cruel world. A weaponless soldier fighting for his life. Once I had everything I thought I needed, whole, my life as I saw it.

Blinded with a curse that came from within. A curse that smiles in your face and gives you a cape to fly. No man can relate. For once you've lost a lifelong friend your destiny becomes failure and your dreams broken.

Resistance becomes an everyday trail. Regret becomes the very thing you breathe. A new beginning from ground zero, the way up seems impossible for the skyscraper is smooth with blood and tears.

You never imagine life can take such an ugly turn and after the crash you see your reflection in the driver's seat.

CHAPTER 4

ANGER < RAGE < BITTERNESS

I shut out most everyone I knew after my life spiraled down. I trusted no one and paranoia took over my mind. I would think people were trying to kill me at my own gym. If someone asked for my number or address it would turn it into an investigation. I would think Rachel wasn't who she said and then wouldn't want to talk to her because I thought she was hiding things from me, even though I was the spy. I hated my friends, they were dead to me. Honestly the only thing keeping me from pulling the trigger were my kids. I held them higher then myself even though bonding with them had not occurred. I had so much hate and anger inside that I would vibrate all over my body. It would feel like someone was stepping on my chest at night. Road rage was at an all time high, and thank God I didn't live far from my gym. My kids, my kids, my kids. Every time I wanted to do something prison worthy they would stop it, but the bitterness didn't end there. I can't tell you how many people would say you're so bitter, and I would respond with a threat. Everything out of my mouth was negative. I wasn't fun to be around; I wanted to go die alone on a rock. The guilt hasn't even hit me yet, that would come later. I would hit the steering wheel till my knuckles bled, and then put a smile on my face right after. It was bordering many things that could ruin my life, but Rachel figured it out just in time. The anger and bitterness was always surfaced while the rage would lay dormant until the alcohol would fill my stomach. There was one instance when I tried turning the steering wheel from the back seat and then jumping out of the car going 40mph. All because of something someone said to me that made me mad. This was typical mood response when I was unstable. Once the medication was in my system the behavior issues vanished, but I kept track through words and paper.

The Thorn

To love someone is to set them free, so I will bolt your wings on and be the nudge
you need as freedom drowns your taste buds. I will splatter a rainbow of red on
these walls that hold you hostage for bondage is what I've built throughout this
home.

I hold you tight in this broken bed, for it murk's pain and sorrow as we laugh
ourselves into ecstasy. A thorn in your side that will spill your insides when the
word revelations awakes from my throat.

I'm poison you've drank, a drug you breathe, for after time my presence will bring
on heartbreak, while torture rests upon your eyelids. I'm your medicine, your sleep
aid, your elixir of life, for one day you'll sleep forever with the remedy that is
me. Embrace my gifts, savor my taste for once I'm gone insanity will seem your
comfort.

I devour you off a gold spoon for your riches have turned my eyes green. In years
I will burn this safe house from within using gasoline that drips from your scalp.
We see eye to eye but live mouth to foot, for envy and jealousy have become my
entourage. I bathe you in silk, lather you with furs, bask you with diamonds and
all you'll see is my honesty and dedication. But I promise you this, I am hollow,
bare with scars from my mother, as my true intentions unfold behind your impaled
back.

To love someone is to let them go, but my love burns too cold and my grip is
slipping, for your heart is worth saving so reach for me no more, break these chains
and let me walk off this cliff. Dry winds, stale air, as you watch your heart walk
into the red sunset. I've saved you, time will mend you, and now peace is what I
leave you with.

The Demon

Deep inside our lungs we breathe him, deep in our mind we create him. He dwells
in us, sleeping cozy in our chest.
He sees thru our pupils as drool hangs off his
weightless chin. He crouches for the race
as liquor is poured at the finish line.
He explodes on the track leaving
bloody footprints in the wet
mud.

He imprisons our body while he strikes the innocent with his heavy bladed
hammer. His presence is too strong
for the mortal, and his yell, too extreme to listen
rationally. We are possessed until he tires
and the ashes fall to his feet.
He crawls back into his
cavity as hell has
left its mark.

To relinquish him is to look the horror in its eyes, strike him down with a sword
made of honesty and grief. Battle him we must as he screams insanity to our face.
He has become us, as claws stem through
our fingertips and reach for our
own neck. We shall rid
of his murky presence
with boldness
　　　　buried deep in our liver,
　　　　　　for the world is a rainbow,
　　　　　　　　and with our demon
　　　　　　　　　　everything is grey.

Scorpions

*Her eyes fill with jealousy as a blood soaked heart begins to
race. Her pupils read death but her tongue drips silence.
A raged filled monster no bigger than a fist becomes lethal with
a single strike from her flawless mouth. Love she no longer feels
for a thick shell made of dragon's skin protects her in loves war.
She moves quickly, outsmarting her prey, leaving them
paralyzed to watch chaos break the walls you've stained green.
Quickly can she turn for another's wrong doing will be justified
with a pierce from her black blade as her neck cannot turn
backwards to watch death harass us.
Her yell, only heard by the underworld, leaves you stiff and
cold, forgetting your future and keeping you frozen in time.
Gentle creatures by nature but with a killer instinct built into
their DNA.
They remain loyal through the worst monsoons and stay true
sacrificing their own needs for your greedy nature.
They hold us close, giving us hope for we indulge in their life's
riches.
They will be your best friend masked with your worst enemy.
Keep them close as if they were gold, keep them fed or feel life's
worst sting. The Scorpio*

The cheek that bleeds

My hands lock with a dainty throat for the last time, for I suffocate you like a rabid animal. Your smooth skin I will bruise no more, for the cost of love is made of tears from a broken past.

No longer will I haunt your dreams or spill your blood, for my heart beats as one with yours. My friend you are, my best friend you are becoming. Every red knuckle that skins your body will cease in time.

Bruised lungs will heal as will your visions of torture. You're best to me as I'm poison for you, as you greet my insanity and cuddle it tight. No longer will I bite the hand that feeds me, no longer will I lay this angered hand upon your cheek.

I break you as I stare hatred into those pretty hazel eyes, they tear for I become the very thing you tried to escape, and in that moment we are unknown.

Never again will I be a stranger, never again will I scar you, never again will I be someone you loath.

Love me for I have good in me, rip kindness from my core as I have from yours, seek and you shall find. Wait and I shall swallow you whole.

Behind Closed Doors

If one man can conquer the world then why can't he conquer himself? If we are all designed the same in theory then why are we so different and unique in our own ways. When we turn to instinct to guide us, is there really such a thing for humans. If a tsunami hit this dark land would we all run or would some stay behind to be captured by the weightless monster. We are all designed to learn and adapt but throughout history civilizations have vanished, for it is said only the strongest survive. But as beings we have the ability to gain strength and evolve for our survival, only to see it ripped from our very feet in seconds with nature's monsters. Why then do some of us give up and exit this world with a sweet bang, when survival is our program. The dawn of man came without record, and the end of man will be in essence without note. Therefore we can never know the true meaning of existence. Are we here to serve a god or do we just simply exist? What purpose to life is there if religion were not an option? Murder, rape, suicide, none of it would truly matter if there is no punishment after this life for we are slaves to no one and our actions hold no consequence if we are without trace. Rewards await those who are righteous and just in this life for an eternal life beyond this one can be yours if you believe it. Temptations of lust and evil wait in the shadows all around us, those who look for them will find them with ease, those who are blind will never turn to the dark side, and those who see with their hearts will have an invisible shield that no demon can touch. We can save others, help those in need and end those who wish it upon themselves. We are built with a complex design structure and with this very tongue we can command an army, with these very hands we can build an empire, and with our hearts we can care for something so deeply with enough envy and hate that we would wage war. Fragile is the end result, with one swift swing of a sword we are obliviated, one wrong step we can break, one wrong swallow and our lunges cease breath from our body. Interesting how something so complex is really so simple and candid. We take for granted what is rightfully ours. Some may see the world with their own eyes and never know what's righteously behind the invisible curtain for those are the unlucky ones. Some may view the world with their hearts and read between the lines, see pheromones blowing in the wind, see love for what it really is, a beautiful curse. Others may see the world without vision, without love or remorse, they may only know sadness and bring to others what they fear the most, happiness. The rare few who can see the world in all its heinous colors and breathe in its life are those who look beyond the closed door, those who reach past the handle and grasp for rarity. We, who see the world through the eyes of our soul, are the ones who truly live and relive.

My Best Friends

The mornings grow cold as my fist paints my feelings on a wall to thin to hold my casket. A bloody sunrise for a sleepless vampire as thoughts of death caffeinate my blood. My neck aches from a dream that is my nightmare in a world that sheds no light on a truth born a lie. My body is heavy with disgust, for my loved ones are surrounded with deceit that has prompted from my teachings.

Dusk plants a craving of a scent that relinquishes the most vial animal, as it hatches in my brain leaving yoke dripping from my eyelids. Exhaustion I have learned to endure, as this world is a disappointment. I see no good, I hear no evil, but my future sings both.
My best friends, my brothers in arms for murder rests on one another's fingertip. Believed in sacrifice for youth as we give our flesh for one another but my map reads an alternate ending.

The neck snaps like a sick tree branch as the morning dew kisses my face and the melody of life sings with empathy. The pulse races, the skin warms like an orange summer day as the red liquid inside splashes the ground with laughter. The earth stops spinning for a brief moment and my insides are numb with ecstasy. Slow is a word not known when it hugs you tight while you fade quickly as the blood slowly fills your lunges and casts a glimpse into your sixty second future.

Clueless in the shadows, they remain my enemy as my flesh speaks friendliness. My standards grow empty with invisible silver stars. Betrayal seems just, for under my wing I place them, masking my face with honestly. I keep them smiling for we shake hands to bond us, but one day I will speak my truth and their answer shall be silence for my blade is an instrument of beauty as I paint their last words on my casket.

Midnight

Midnight. Blood scales down his hands but reads of another's DNA. The exhaust from his mouth is dense. His heart steady as his mind finds serenity. Once two now one, he takes the pride of justice as his own. A tingle dances up his spine, while a sigh of relief stems from his corrupt soul.

11pm. A rapid train carrying flesh and bones moves through his valiant mind. He sees the finale before it is written. A massacre painted on a brilliant white canvas. Sweat and anxiety burry his lungs, exhaustion floods his mind but sharp his eyes remain. He sees the line of damnation, crawling over it but never looking back, for now he holds the key to the pearly white gates. All powerful reads his name, for he has been reborn from the reapers womb.

4pm. Heartache enters his faultless world. She never loved him. She is bred for another but love sick he has become. Vomiting memories from an empty bottle that breaks into a vision death. Paralyzed with the floor, he dreams a solution to an impossible equation. Jealousy swells in his tears as he musters up courage. The reaper will become him, his life for another's, for midnight will spell revenge.

Spiders

You trap us like flies born blind into this wintery world, for we cannot see your castle in the dark. You spin but never move, while you create your disposable masterpiece. You take your time knowing we will come, following the animalistic scent you left behind.

We run to you like skinless dogs, our mouths hanging open with the taste of your flesh on our tongues as we approach the mirage. Standing there with eight legs but only two visible as they drip death. Your touch feels like an angel shed their skin with a chainsaw and melted it to our faces. We are paralyzed without time as your bite of lust has turned fatal.

Your eyes transform us, for you see all four of our shapes and personalities. You know us before you've met us, and are confident in your disposal. The poison hits hard but we fall soft, we are still alive, but we cannot breathe, we see you but your mask is off. The horrors unfold and deep into the coma we journey for you have released us from pain and misery, giving us eternity.

We are food for a disturbed appetite that we have forged since the beginning of time. Cozy in their corners, as they can tell no lie behind the magic they weave, they can only mask it with fear.

We can crush them, we can fire back but they bite us while we sleep, they sink their fangs in when we turn our backs and disturb the natural flow. They will leave our half eaten corpse hanging for the whole world to see for this is what you get when you betray the queen.

The Darkness

The darkness, a concoction of liquor and rage. We burry it deep in inside
while the vultures circle our heads
and wait for its remains. It stems from scars,
and awakens from haunted memories
killing any future in its way.

The darkness will see you with elusive eyes, burning a hole through trust
and ripping apart your sanity.
Glass shatters, walls bruise, and utensils
becomes weapons.

Possessed we have become, for our loved ones are now prey in a forest
caught on fire with our own match.
We hunt our partner with silence while chaos emotes from our lips.

Nothing can stop the beast, nowhere to hide for anxiety and confusion
entraps us in a small white room.
Threats mandate, while choice flees.

Save our loved one engorged with this demon or run and let the earth
crumble behind us.

Help is spelled backwards as tears are filled with betrayal.
One's own life matters not as the jagged edges silence
the raging beast
as breath ceases from their body.

We tried to love them, we tried to bury them with happiness, but in
return, a cold kiss from deaths lips.

My Reflection

You've taken my hand while leading my broken remains into a mansion of prosperity, while the other rots gently with mine for your hood and mask smell of horror.

You've shown me a new path built with stainless steel and porcelain, for we walk on bones and skulls that are secret to the world as they lay 2fold in their undecided graves.

You calm me when I exasperate, you keep my heart from pulsing out of my mouth, while you are the one who initially set the blade and forced my hand to cut as my mind numbed and I lost myself in innocent wide eyes.

Language you've studied with me, for we can speak any dialect to create illusion. You've led me to the top of the mountain, where rivers flow and fruit melts in your tan hands, but it came with the price of my holy ghost for you now wear it draped around your boneless body.

You've listened to me as my face covered in red tears and body bruised with confusion. We have the same reflection but I only see purple teeth and red eyes for the mirror on the wall can tell no lie.

I am you, and you are what has become of me, for I am your creation, a lab rat your experiment sufficed with.

I bleed green and drink from the sewers, as you stalk from above flagging me down as dinner approaches, for we starve ourselves to insanity.

My kingdom, your lair, together we are gods enemy in this wasteland of treasure, for we spawned from our mother but shall die from each other, for one day I will rip the head from this monster that is I . . .

CHAPTER 5

REDEMPTION

The second Rachel figured out I was bi polar she sought help for me; bless her soul because if those pills didn't kill me, my index finger would have. You get tired battling your mind and you never win. It weighs on you and you start second guessing if you can fight anymore. I went to a few therapists and psychiatrists. When they would say I was bi polar I looked at them like they were crazy. One day I was on my way to an appointment and a car hit mine pretty hard. I got out and yelled at the guy and said "what the f is wrong with you, I have an appointment now get the hell out of my way." I told the psychiatrist off as well about three times before I actually listened and tried lithium. Changed my life. My last crazy "manicsode" would end with Hawaii and sky diving with 102 fever the same day we arrived. I also would hear noises when I was manic, it was one noise actually and it sounded like a shield from a military video game losing power. I would hear it at the beach, in a quiet room, in the car, etc. It would bring me to tears because I thought this is it I'm going crazy. When the lithium finally slowed me down after about 4 months I was consistent. I felt great and I saw my life could be more normal. I still go through the cycles even on lithium but nowhere close to what they use to be. A typical "manicsode" will be something where I want to buy material or sign up for something crazy which I can control every time now because I can think clearly, and finally sleep!!!! Depression is faint and over quick now, I don't really even notice it. I'm finally the father my family always wanted and the friend she always needed. My family is my life and I always wonder what would have happened if we found out sooner, I guess it's a question that will always haunt me. The battle is finally over and it's great to be looking at the peak again and at the same time that journey would be documented through words.

Cinnamon

The apple of my eye, the cinnamon on my tongue, for your bite leaves my
neck full of raw honey.
We bathe in wine while grapes fall from our invisible vineyard. Your skin
resembles brandy in the sunlight, your eyes daze me for they stick on me like
caramel.

You set me on fire while the drool from your lips turns into steam and my
body melts into yours.
My face you lash as the tears run down your throat, for your delicate hand
holds both fear and comfort. A powdered baby I shall remain for my
innocence feeds the animal in you, while my youth takes for granted the queen
you are.

Dancing in the moonlight as we remember raindrops of bliss that filled our
passionate souls with hope.
I give you what's left of me as my body sweats on top yours, while you let my
hand squeeze the life from your exhausted lungs.
I loved you into this world we created as I will weep with love as I watch you
exit, for my intensions are pure with evil.

A free spirit once, a broken soul twice and now your mind I've devoured into
cinnamon, for that is the taste that will reside on my tongue as I command
you into the underworld.
Love was a bubble we popped with our slurs of jealousy as the gum stuck to
our faces. Shallow is my lake as you've poured your insides to fill it. Drown
we will for my raft is made of sticks and string that I've tied together blindly.

I have no honey to drip, I have no passion to build, I am a robot
programmed with a blank disc, for you are the one who built me. I beg and
plead happiness but my words vanish as the rabbit flees my hat.
One day you will find me. One day you will become pure. One day you will
rip apart my insides and fill them with yours and loves beat will warm my
chest once more.

Eye of the Dragon

Dark eyes of ancient dragons dwell within a broken mans soul, giving him the power to see through any wall of emotion. Guarded treasures now seem to find him, he no longer needs his hand of solitude for his conscious is made of raw flesh and salvaged tear drops.

He has bled his heart dry and cut his soul free, as for now he can live in peace. The demons of his past no longer linger in the shadows, they weep in the distance as their cries are heard but not obliged. He's longed for happiness in a nightmare that will taste a new reality as his mind breaks free from the tyrant that wears his cape.

Born in a doubt filled world, raised by his own hand, as his ambitions soak him in gasoline while he is reborn through his fiery eyes. His body cleansed of evil, his mind blessed with time, and his heart pieced together from its shattered remains. He now can see the world for its beauty and integrity within. A man almost buried, now healing through the bond of love can see a future he only dreamed of.

He journeys through the Black Sea as the clouds pamper his skin. He reaches a foreign shore but has seen it before. A castle with dragons spells and witches. He enters knowing he will slay them all for they are him from the past, for his future will be cleansed with his blood.

History repeats when our ears do not listen, as men fall when they repeat history, so he writes his book with the ghost of his past so he can taste the horrors that dwelled in this castle as he devours them. Sleeping atop, his dark princess awaits rescue from her prince as she has never aged a day. Rule this foreign kingdom he will. Reclaim glory he must or perish in its name.

The Holy Knight

I've slain the green dragon and burned his head whole. I've tasted your wine as it drizzled off your porcelain feet. I've trespassed through the stone fortress in which you lay captured, as my sword guts any mortal in my path.

Rescue you I must, for your beauty has cursed 1000 souls. I've never laid eyes upon your face but legend tells it was painted by the gods.

I've seen war a hundred times, I've witnessed men die at my feet, I've felt brothers aim their blade at my back for I bear no hesitation in watching betrayal spew from their throat as my feet soak in blood.

Your tale is worth dying to discover. Many say you are haunted, many tell stories that portray a lustful past life, but none can say they've ever held your beating heart.

I will seek you, I will have you, I will destroy this earth to find you. You've came to me in my dreams, torturing me with your very breath as it whispered hope in my twisted mind. I cannot contain you, for you may not be real.

I cannot love you for my heart knows no ghost. Your heart will be mine, as I slice the hands from time and create you. I shall have vengeance in this life while I skin your body of scars, and cut you open to bleed dry the black blood inside your veins.

Replenished you will remain, holy is the venom that now runs through you. Reborn my will has made you, visions of life now embrace you, as for now I can finally lay my armor down and know you. For I have created you.

A Message To Earth

My love, my lost mate for your half eaten soul resides on earth. I leave you this from beyond our world and its contaminated contents. I've seen wonders, brilliance only a dead man's eyes can bear. I've watched you grow as grace has become your fuel for a fire that burns deep in your heart, for I am no longer your cherished one.

My memories come alive in this place as your kiss is my breakfast at a table that holds your young body for I only see us in youth. Bring my sons knowledge for my words only scare them, bring them warmth for I am chills, whisper hope that one day I will greet them upon the golden gates.

I am frozen in time, a memory that drips off a cheek.
You'll feel me when the wind blows and the trees sing our song. My presence fills you, for part of you is twined with me but I'm weightless. The air I breathe is nothing but bliss, and for every breath I take my world gets smaller and grey. I find you when my spirit breaks and screams your ghost, but you are trapped in rotting flesh that imprisons our true love.

I shall wait for eternity to have you, as I sit in this portrait of blood that my wrists have painted. A cowardly exit, but my heart would no longer beat in pieces. I shall return but in a different form, though my soul will have your scent. I will seek what is lost and make you believe in miracles, for I forged one from Gods hand for love is above dying as I race to earth to be reborn.

Balance

Visions of you never cease in a mind that never rests. Balance is what you are. Stability is what you bring. Love is what you breathe. And with every breath you capture a piece of my very soul.

In an endless battle you are the embassy, the bomb shelter that is indestructible, the safe haven in a world with no sun or air.

You bring light to the darkest places, places where we never sleep or age, places where monsters are born and enemies become fathers, places where unimaginable things are your sweetest dreams.

You are the sword that slayed the four eyed monster, your body tattooed with his blood forever, and your skin bonded with his ghost.

Forever will you be my shield, my fortress where I can rest and happiness is only a footstep away, overlooking a sea of elusive dreams.
No one person can say loneliness is part of them. No one person can say bonded forever will they be for ones future isn't determined by will but fate itself. Staring us in the face our entire lives waiting to strike and alter history.

With a sword and shield one has a chance of fighting and staying whole. Without it, we have already lost.

Running in Place

For the first time in my life, I am still. Nothing you throw can move me, nothing you spit can shake me for I am solid in a world filled with liquid. My feet planted deep in the dusty ground, my body covered in titanium, and my skull layered thrice.

You've broken me once, you've twisted me twice and a million scars are what you left on my fragile insides. No longer will I be the victim, no longer will you blind me for your gentle speech impairs the dark lord himself.

I wish to heal you, I wish to save the remains of your soul that are pure, and create with you a life we can smile at. So long has this frown kept me from the fast lane, so long we have fibbed sweet nothings in a mind that can only listen but never promote. We are poison, we are venom that strikes with a soft touch.

Run I will not, for you cannot chase what doesn't move. I will be your foundation built on new trust for everything old is tainted with disease. I will show you a life only few have savored, and give you comfort many have only felt in a womb.

I will never flee for we are antidote to venom we've spewed at each other in a past I can't remember. Solid I have become for your pain has built me, stable I rest for your tears have conditioned me, above you I will never climb for we will be each other's equals.

Only next to you I shall remain as we feed off pure energy from broken souls as we twinkle under the blue stars.

My love. My dearest, my hand will always lay across your beaded chest as we dream of a future discarded of a past we once lived.

Pursuit Of Happiness

Happiness, the very thing that has no price. We cannot buy it in a store or steal it off a wrinkled neck. We cannot see it in a sunset, nor hear it in song. Money can burn but the tears we cry will never spark a rainbow. We lust for its touch but are whipped until our spines dangle from our skin.

We pay off debt and somehow owe more into this enslavement we call government. We run through the desert with a shirt of thorns and at the checkered flag our blood paints no smile.

We suffer to achieve greatness when you will never reach satisfaction. Dreams of the color bliss are no match for the color envy as our paintbrush is spun by more than one hand. We speak of it, but no one listens, we scream with it, but no one looks twice, for happiness is only reached when one can love themselves.

We spit in the faces of those who are negative signs in our positive equation. We will be bold; we will stand our ground, as the sadness of the world plays though television and newspaper trying to sell us a story that our ears will ooze from.

Armor is thick and our heart beats powerfully so long as the world throws its bullets and shoots its trains through our house of redemption.

Happiness, a word not reached by many, a word forgotten by most, a word that should be spoken with caution for one's mind is not born with it, it must be earned.

The Forbidden Forest

It holds what we seek and forgives what we sowed. The future bears treasures a mortal mind does not comprehend. We read it in books, spend it with money, and search for it with time. Our past can be dark as the forecast ahead is beaming with light. Monsters gallop close behind as we sprint for a fresh start.

Everything we dream, everything we imagine is sitting before our eyes, it parades on a gold street with trumpets calling our name. Before we reach it we must break ties with those who bear weight around a chained ankle.

Cut them down like a rabid dog we must, for they hold no glory in our upcoming journey. Rid of dark habits, gone with our lustful eyes, as we smash everything black and saw from our skull those beady pupils that only see in red.

Trek thru the forest of tears and fire for we will weep as our old flesh burns. Leaving us in a deathly state but pushing us into bliss. Patience as we exit the other side, many will not recognize who we have become as our skin glows and eyes fill with life.

Only those closest see the miracle, for we are now a holy breed of a once lost mind. We see in bright white, we feel with love, and we now can put those who we cherish on a pedestal higher then ourselves.
Forbidden is the forest of solitude as ones journey has not begun. For it is written, ones quest to bliss can only begin when one's life is about to end.

For You

You hold the key to unlocking my drive, with which I will crush everything in my vision. You store a chest that holds ancient secrets a weak mind would crumble from. You wear a locket around that soft pulsed throat, from which my broken heart hangs off.

You've given me your life as I gnawed on its remains and showed you love from a different breed. You sacrificed time for me as I sped up the clock for doomsday. You gave me your innocence as I burned mine before your eyes.

For you,
I shall die without a second glance and lay my body down as the world tramples and rapes it so I can see you untouched. I will look death in the face for the first and last time as you run far from a battle my subconscious has created.

For you
I cut out my heart and keep it safe so after yours shatters you remain whole. I sleep under a bridge so that you may walk on clouds. I will keep you safe when my cape flows with my storm, and protect you against scum who wear suits and mask a warped face with a white smile.

You've shown me unconditional love, and embraced every wound from a rusted blade held in my pocket. I will never let you down again, I will make your name eternal, I will love you behind a brick wall and give you the part of me you loved best. A masked villain I must remain, for to see you blossom I must die in the shadows.

The Lost Fight

Her death bed is made of pink lilies, as she climbs willingly abroad. She lays there still as her memories sprint wild. She was my pearl in this greedy oyster we call earth. She thinks of him only in their youth for in a time of purity he beamed light. She leans into him and whispers,
fight for me.
Flashbacks swarm, whirl pooling around his almost bald head as 2012 replays its ghost. Young and solid we were for in a time of doubt she was my rock. I spent my later years showering a once known gem with gifts only my fortune could buy, for my guilt outweighed the other 36 emotions. We separated premature as our hearts tore apart and a cold chill was the only thing remaining. 2 beautiful offspring we left behind as our legacy would now shadow through them.
Fight for me,
echoed in a twisted mind, readied with a pocket knife and pistol to face the horrors trapped in midnight. I knew it was a battle already lost for I could not alter myself single handedly. She pleaded change, I longed for it, but together doom was my motivation.
Fight for me.
Words that didn't make sense, a sentence that read in Egyptian for I could not crack the code. Simple her life was, messy it would become, as times hand would heal her as I faded from it.
The pink lilies smelled of new life, as my hand held hers with a touch known from a stranger. Friends we remained as life's clock winded down for the two of us. Separate lives we made, new memories now filled our intake as the old ones were locked in a 1000lb safe. Regret was a word unknown and guilt had faded with material things.
My love for her had never died as I saw it through my boy's eyes.
Sword less and nude was how I entered the battle for her, and best it remains, for never fighting was the greatest gift I ever bestowed upon her. Walking hand and hand with a monster is living life in a shadow. So I slayed myself and set her free.

Skydive Hawaii with 102 fever

Kitchen to our first home

A month later

Brutus who I let go after 7 years

Logan my son resting after the crash cart miracle birth

India – hotel view

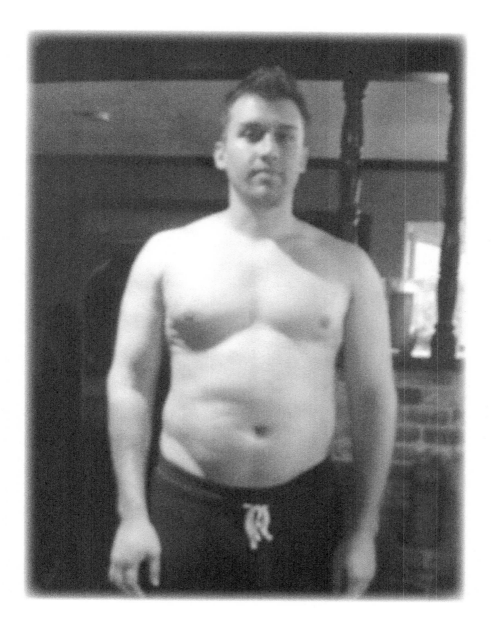

A week before the India trip 249lbs

6 weeks after India 205lbs

My company – Lift

Pasadena lift

Rancho lift

Covina lift

Expansion Covina lift – group room

Me and my boys enjoying life

Rachel and me

Made in the USA
Monee, IL
17 May 2022

96610505R00049